Cognitive Behavioral Therapy 101

Mind Exercises and Techniques:

Simple Ways to Retrain your Brain to Overcome Anxiety, Phobias, and Depression

Kasey Wittmann

Table of Contents

Characteristics of Cognitive Behavioral Therapy

Cognitive Behavioral Therapy (CBT) is a psychiatric treatment intended to convert a person's disoriented emotions into positive emotions in order to achieve a healthy state of mind. CBT works to treat a wide array of psychological therapeutic techniques, with each having its own unique approach.

Basic concept behind Cognitive Behavioral Therapy

The theory behind CBT is that a person's emotions, feelings or behavior are a result of their own personal analysis of a stimulant. Feelings or thoughts about certain events or situations might emerge organically, no matter how negative and erroneous they are. Such thoughts eventually lead to depression and anxiety: CBT teaches people how to notice when this negativity is coming so that they can alter their views to something healthier and more realistic, without drastically changing the circumstance.

There are various types of Cognitive Behavioral Therapy treatments, but the majority of them have these same following characteristics.

1. CBT treatments are centered on the theory that an individual's thoughts, not outer influences, define their behavior and emotions. This is considered a plus, since it grants people the ability to change the way they view a certain stimulant and therefore accommodate their behavior to react positively without the need of changing the stimulant.

2. CBT produces quicker results and is done within a specific timeframe. CBT on average lasts 16 sessions, with the objective of achieving drastic improvement in a very short timeframe. In the early stages of treatment, the patient will be informed that the process will not carry on indefinitely, and standard therapy will end after a certain length of time. After each session, the patient will receive homework related to their experiences to speed up the therapy.

3. While a trusting and constructive relationship between the therapist and patient is a requisite feature of CBT, the role of the therapist is not simply to advise the patient, but also to teach them how to process their thoughts and emotions in a rational and calm manner.

4. CBT is structured and complies with a standard system. Each session will focus on it's own specific procedure where concepts and techniques are taught which are meant to have the patient figure out how to achieve their goals, and what behaviors they should adopt in order to achieve said goals.

Hands-on application of the concepts and methods learned in CBT are meant to expose the patient to their amplified response to certain situations and teach them more effective and reasonable ways to channel their thoughts. CBT is very effective in reducing anxiety disorder symptoms and is frequently used in the place of anti-depressants. CBT is also an essential part of drug rehabilitation therapy, insomnia treatment, and to offer pain relief to the elderly who suffer from arthritis.

The concept behind Cognitive Behavioral Therapy

The goal of every CBT therapist is to teach their patients to become more aware of their emotions, thoughts, and beliefs about their problems. The therapist helps point out inconsistent beliefs and thought patterns that enhance the problem.

After that, the therapist helps people question their illogical and pessimistic thoughts by offering alternative opinions and perusing them to adopt a different point of view. Therapists typically provide viewpoints that help patients look for the overall probability of certain issues and generalizations. For example, a person who insists that "People don't like me," might be asked by their therapist, "Did you ever confirm with someone that they didn't like you?"

How it works

CBT sessions are constructed based on an individual's needs. Therefore, it can take many forms to suit the needs of a patient. Each CBT session has a common element: patients and therapists collaborate and work together to discover the best approach to a problem. The process of CBT is as follows:

1. Discovering the belief, thought, or process that needs attention

2. Determining which method is best to modify the belief system or behavior

3. Making assumptions about the outcome and crafting a way to document it

4. Thinking about challenges and how to overcome them through an experiment

5. Performing the experiment

6. Analyzing the results

7. Discovering follow-up experiments if required

The therapist and the patient collaborate closely to craft the experiment. After this initial stage, the patient experiments and tracks the results. And finally, the therapist and client reflect on the impact that said experiment had.

CBT examples

Overall, therapists can aid individuals in dealing with and managing a wide array of problems. Some of the most frequent behavioral experiments are:

1. A lady thinks the only way in which a group of people will like her is if she is perfect at all times. As a result, this perfectionism encourages feelings of anxiety and

stress. A behavioral experiment for her might be placing her in a situation in which she makes mistakes on purpose. After she analyses the outcome, she will discover that people won't respond as badly as she might expect.

2. A man has convinced himself that he is an introvert. As a result, he avoids any social encounter, or he distances himself as far away as possible from a group of people. A behavioral experiment for him might be attending a social gathering weekly and trying to interact with at least four people. In the end, he will realize that people were very welcoming when he is friendly.

3. A woman is obsessed with her fiancée cheating. So, she spends a lot of time on social media platforms to track his steps. A behavioral experiment for her might be avoiding social media for several weeks so that she sees if her anxiety decreases.

How Cognitive Behavior Therapy Works

Cognitive-behavioral therapy can significantly improve your quality of life. Hence, if you decided it is time to explore CBT, this article is for you. Next, we've shared the basics behind CBT, along with what you should expect during this type of therapy.

CBT basics

The first thing you need to do is research and identify a good CBT therapist. The goal is to trust him or her to create a stable therapeutic relationship. It is highly recommended to unload with as many questions as possible during your first session. For example, you can ask about their therapeutic approach or how they implement CBT in their sessions.

Keep in mind that this first therapy session is meant to offer insights on what your long-term goals should be. Your therapist will discuss the issues you will have to work with. Hence, it is best to be open about your problems and goals, so the CBT sessions have optimal benefits. The more information your therapist gathers in the first session, the more likely they will be able to tailor an individual treatment plan for you.

Committing to CBT sessions

After this initial meeting with your therapist, you will create a foundation of facts and approaches with each visit. This means that every therapy session will start with a thorough analysis of your last visit. And you and your therapist will pick out the subject you will discuss in your session. An average CBT session consists of the following:

1. Analyzing and discovering the issue

2. Sharing your feelings and beliefs concerning the situation that triggered the problem

3. Identifying negative thoughts or behaviors

4. Addressing negative thinking

Keep in mind that your therapist won't get you through all these steps at once. Instead, they will guide you towards gaining awareness about your situation or problem.

CBT homework

You mean there's homework?! Yes. The assignments are meant to enable you to see how your feelings or actions impact your day to day life. As an example, you might have to document how your depression, OCD, or anxiety manifests daily. And based on this data, your therapist might suggest an exercise meant to help you manage the symptoms. In the following session, you will share your insights and results with your therapist.

Discovering new techniques

An essential part of CBT therapy is understanding and learning the skills necessary to help you deal with your problems. There are distinct approaches to this, including:

- Performing exercises that help you achieve relaxation and calmness

- Implementing stress management techniques

- Understanding and discovering strategies that can assist you in analyzing an issue and identifying the solution

Keep in mind that such approaches can consist of a significant part of your homework. So, you might have to experiment with the relaxation techniques at home and then a new technique in the following week.

CBT group sessions

Cognitive-behavioral therapy is constructed to work as an individual therapy approach. There are several situations in which it can function better in a group. Group therapy offers emotional support and is a safe environment where you can share your vulnerabilities. In addition, the participants in this session can provide their support and advice in regards to shared experiences.

Cognitive-behavioral therapy represents an efficient treatment approach that can help one in dealing with numerous issues. The main benefit that you will receive from these sessions is the fact that you will be taught new self-care skills. Additionally, you will gain more confidence after each completed assignment.

How Cognitive Behavioral Therapy Can Help With the Negative Thoughts

Research has shown that CBT can significantly help with fighting depression. During CBT sessions, you will work with your therapist to find a common ground on behavior patterns that need to be improved. The aim is to rewire the part of your brain that's got a such a tight grasp on positive thoughts.

Frequent CBT sessions and homework can help strengthen new and positive patterns. Once you learn to recognize those negative thoughts and put them behind you, you will feel very liberated.

CBT Techniques to Counteract the Negative Thinking of Depression

The problem with self-study and homework is that those with depression rarely respond well to it. For this reason, it is recommended that, if you are currently afflicted with depression, to commit to CBT therapy for a minimum of six weeks. Your therapist will prioritize CBT techniques that can help combat the negative thinking patterns linked to depression. He or she will also make sure you stick to the plan and practice your techniques. Here are five CBT techniques you may carry out with your therapist:

A benchmark of depression is hopelessness — an uncertainty that your life will get any better. Create a list of things you know will better a situation to help reduce your depression. For example, if you are feeling lonely, a solution might be to join a club in your town that caters to your interest or sign up for a local charity group.

Identify the problem and work out solutions.

Talking with your therapist and journaling can help lead you to the source of your depression. Once you come to a realization, journal your thoughts in a small sentence, acknowledging what is causing you pain and come up with ways to mend the issue.

Remember your reflections and relay them back to yourself when your mind starts to nest out a negative thought. Over time, you will build new conjunctions, superseding old negative thoughts with new positive ones.

Your self-reflection should not be too removed from any negative thoughts, or your mind might reject it. For example, if you are thinking, "My life is so depressing," instead of telling yourself, "Nothing is wrong with my life," a better message might be, "Every person has ups and downs in their lives, and I am not exempt of this rule." This statement reassures you that it's fine to feel a healthy degree of happiness in your life. By the same token, your mind rewards itself for focusing on happiness to shield from depression.

Sometimes self-reflections become too repetitive and require creative thinking. It is recommended to rephrase them, translate them into other languages you may speak, possibly even making them sound more joyful. For example, a self-reflection like "It's okay to embrace my ups" can become "It's great that I am having a super "up" day today."

Seek opportunities that encourage positive thinking

People who arrive somewhere and immediately think. "That wall color is ugly," should instead condition themselves to focus on the things in the area that they might like as fast as possible. Set an alarm on your phone three times a day to remind you to readjust your thinking patterns into something positive. It's also a good idea to "buddy-up" with another person practicing the same technique. This way, you can encourage each other to think positively about your experiences and share your opinions throughout the day.

End your day by recalling its best parts

At the end of your day, write in a journal everything you are grateful for in life. Documenting positive thoughts can help your mind create new conjunctions or create new pathways. A person who's opened up a new pathway of thinking may go from getting up in the morning and thinking, "Ugh, I hate going to work" to "I can't wait to start the day."

Learn to accept failures as an everyday part of life

Failures are an inevitable part of life, and your reaction to those stumbles can affect your ability to get over them. Someone experiencing a breakup might feel guilt over it or even gain weight, thinking, "Why bother looking good? No one will ever want to be with me." A healthier approach may be to permit yourself to feel the pain of your failures and remember that you cannot control everything that happens. Work on the things that you can control: Write down the experiences, what you learned from them, and the things you can do next time to avoid these stumbles. This can help you develop a more positive outlook for your future.

Cognitive Behavioral Therapy Strategies

For several years, many specialists have focused on analyzing the effects of the main cognitive coping strategies. These include the following: acceptance, blame-gaming, catastrophizing and pre-judging. Below we will go through a summary of the most efficient cognitive-behavioral techniques that can help you manage a wide array of symptoms, including the ones previously mentioned.

Self-monitoring

Self-monitoring is a rather standard cognitive-behavioral coping approach. We can safely say this strategy is the foundation of all coping strategies we mention in this article. Self-monitoring refers to the necessity of becoming aware of our issues. Awareness can enable us to discover the cause of a problem while underlining the path we need to take so that we regain our balance.

Diaphragmatic breathing

Diaphragmatic breathing is also known as abdominal breathing or deep breathing. It is meant to boost oxygen intake and cleanse the body from excess amounts of carbon dioxide. This type of breathing can have a positive impact on your body, as it balances your blood pressure and slows the heartbeat. It is an especially potent cognitive-behavioral coping strategy for those suffering from anxiety.

Progressive muscle relaxation

Progressive Muscle Relaxation or PMR is another efficient deep relaxation approach recommended for managing stress, anxiety, insomnia, and chronic pain. The core principle behind PMR is to intensify your muscle slowly, hold the tension for a couple of seconds, and release it. You will also have to tense your muscles systematically, starting with your toes and working your way up to your body. It has been proven to be an efficient technique for anxiety, as it can teach your body and mind that muscle tension is an indicator you need to relax.

Behavioral activation

Studies show that depressed or anxious individuals lack the desire to participate and indulge in activities they used to love. Hence, it is somewhat necessary to re-discover the joy in specific activities. And behavioral activation is supposed to do that. Its purpose is straightforward: it guides individuals and prompts them to become active in aspects of their lives that can fill them with joy and satisfaction. As a result, this connection with fulfilling activities can drastically increase mental wellbeing.

Decision-making: good vs. bad

Many people feel like having to decide upon a set of choices is a big challenge. And some individuals freeze on this thought and fail to deal with it. But the decision-making coping strategy is meant to help you achieve a more precise perspective about a particular situation. This approach will encourage you to analyze the good and the bad about a situation or decision. And as a result, you can discover the best method for achieving your goals with the smallest risks possible.

Cognitive restructuring

Cognitive restructuring is a process in cognitive behavioral therapy meant to allow you to identify and change negative thoughts. It is beneficial for those aiming to suppress feelings of depression and anxiety. This approach might help you improve your mental and emotional wellbeing, as you will attempt to change your thoughts with the sole purpose of nurturing positive vibes.

Choosing and following goals

We need to have a purpose at all times in our lives. Such goals or desired accomplishments are the ones that offer meaning, security, and a clear path in life. Besides, choosing and following goals can encourage healthy behaviors, which in turn can significantly improve your life. Still, this can prove to be counterproductive if we fail to select a reasonable goal. And as a result, we might feel overwhelmed and unable to accomplish it. It's always best to approach goals gradually and carefully to cause as little stress to your well-being as possible.

How Cognitive Behavioral Therapy Uses Goal Setting

"I need to get physically fit!" "I don't want to work at a dead-end job anymore." "I want to achieve happiness and become a more successful person."

These kinds of statements are likely familiar to us. Most people are good at locating traits or habits we would like to change in our lives. However, carrying out these changes is usually a lot more of a challenge than figuring out what they are. Sometimes we are intimidated by the goal in front of us and afraid to tackle it. Other times, we do our best to try to reach a goal, but things just don't work out. When this happens, it's easy to lose hope and give up.

The good news is, there are techniques that can set you on the right track and help you reach any goal you set your mind to. Conceptualizing a goal can be of great benefit to many aspects of your life, such as:

- reconnecting with friends from the past
- looking for a new job
- taking on a new hobby
- saving for a much-needed vacation
- spending more quality time with a partner

- chores around the home (e.g., cleaning out the basement)

Goal setting can also help improve people's behavioral and emotional difficulties and is a fundamental part of CBT. For example, a person who is depressed might seek therapy to reach the goal of growing the number and bond of their friendships.

A person suffering anxiety due to the intensity of their job may work with their therapist toward seeking a different career or finding some time in their schedule for some leisure and relaxation. Due to the fact that goal setting techniques are often incorporated into CBT, this approach is especially beneficial for people who are having a hard time reaching their goals, no matter what those goals may be.

The following goal setting method consists of the techniques used in CBT but can also help those who do not seek therapy.

- Locate your goal. It might seem simple at first, but finding a clear goal can be challenging. To start, ask yourself, "What is the purpose of my goal?"

- Find your start point. Once you locate your goal, put your current life into perspective in respect to that goal. Be truthful and ask yourself, "How much do I like my current situation?"

Layout the steps. It can be hard to stay on track and remember that achieving a goal is rarely done by taking shortcuts. Keep your goal separated into "blocks" by locating all the steps required to get from your plan's starting point to the goal. Ask yourself, "What are some ways I can simplify the process to make the goal more attainable?"

Keep each step simple and small

Small steps are easier attained than large ones. When you feel the joys of achieving each step gradually, it helps keep you motivated and working towards your end goal. Also, when you pass your small step goal, you will feel proud of yourself for getting on the right path to recovery!

Put the steps in order

Ask yourself, "What should I do to achieve my first step?" and "Will I be ready for the next step?" and so on. Concentrate on the first steps. **Consider possible hurdles.** Think about the things that could throw you off your plan to accomplish the steps you laid out and find workarounds to these problems to your best ability. No one knows how they will deal with potential hurdles, but by taking the time to consider them beforehand, you will be better prepared to work around these problems when they come.

Start with the first step in your action plan

Following these steps will give you the confidence needed to accomplish the goals you set for yourself and make the process much easier to achieve.

Finally, the acronym SMART can be very helpful in setting out your goals and steps appropriately. This stands for:

Specific

Make your steps as specific as possible, so you can know for sure when you have completed a goal or step. "Exercise more" is vague, but "Go walk around the neighborhood 4 times a week" is clear and easier to check off your list of steps

Measurable

Creating measurable steps and goals means you can keep track of your progress. In the previous example, specifying "4 times a week" grants you a reference point to notice the change in your exercising habits.

Achievable

Before choosing a goal make sure it can actually be achieved. It might be great to dream of winning it big in the lottery and becoming mega-rich, but there is a very slim chance you will attain that goal, no matter how much you try to or plan out your steps.

Relevant

Make sure your goal lines up with the problem you are trying to fix. Learning to improve your public speaking abilities is a great goal, but it may not be the most important if your end goal is to make more friends.

Timely

Make sure you pick a good time to start working to achieve your goal. For example, striving to clean out the basement may be a productive goal but probably not wise if you are recovering from knee surgery.

In tackling your goals, if you find yourself unable to finish a particular step in your goal plan, look at it more closely. It is possible you are not minimizing the size of the step well enough, so do not be afraid to simplify it some more and continue from there.

Practicing goal setting techniques takes time to master, but can be an essential tool in helping you to accomplish the things you have been procrastinating or just don't know how to approach. Finding the proper therapist for your needs can be a challenge. Consider scheduling an appointment with a CBT therapist if you are seeking therapy to help you attain your goals.

Cognitive Behavioral Therapy for Anxiety

CBT is the most commonly used therapy method for anxiety disorders. Studies have shown it to greatly reduce the symptoms of phobias, panic disorder, and anxiety disorder, among various other ailments.

CBT confronts negative patterns in how we see ourselves and our surroundings. This involves two main components:

Our thoughts – not physical experiences – affect how we feel. In other words, the situations you experience do not determine your feelings; rather, your perception of the events does. As an example, imagine that you are participating in a big party. Conceptualize three different ways of playing out the event and what kind of effect those thoughts would have on your emotions.

Situation: You find yourself at a big party

Thought #1: This party is great. I love the jubilant feeling of being around lots of happy people!

Emotions: Excited, happy

Thought #2: I am not a party person. I would prefer to stay home and enjoy a nice movie.

Emotions: Neutral

Thought #3: I feel very awkward around so many people having a great time while I am not. I should do everyone else a favor and just go.

Emotions: Anxious, sad

As you can see, dependent on your perspective, the same event can result in entirely different emotions depending on the person. It all hinges on your personal beliefs, attitudes, and expectations. For individuals with anxiety, pessimistic thinking feeds the negative emotions of fear and anxiety. The purpose of CBT therapy for anxiety is to locate and fix these pessimistic thoughts and beliefs. The goal is to change your thinking habits, so you can change how you feel.

Thought challenging in CBT for anxiety

Thought challenging is a procedure in which your negative thinking patterns are challenged and replaced with more realistic, positive thoughts. This consists of three steps:

Locating your negative thoughts

In the case of anxiety disorders, events are made out to be more alarming than they actually are. For example, for a person with a germ phobia, a simple handshake with another person can appear to be life-threatening. Regardless if you recognize that this fear isn't rational, calling out your own irrational, fearsome thoughts is very difficult. One technique is to ask yourself what your thoughts were when you began to feel anxious. Your therapist will help you make these thoughts out if needed.

Confronting your negative thoughts

In this step, your therapist will instruct you on how to analyze your anxiety-triggering thoughts properly. This includes being skeptical of the reasoning for your frightening thoughts, evaluating defeatist beliefs, and testing negative predictions to see their actual results. Techniques for confronting your negative thoughts include weighing the pros and cons of backing out of the thing you are afraid of and evaluating the probability of your feared scenario actually happening.

Substituting negative thoughts with positive, realistic thoughts

Once you have figured out the negative and irrational fears causing your anxious thoughts, you can substitute them with new, more rational and positive thoughts. Your therapist might also guide you in conceptualizing accurate, calming affirmations you can tell yourself in times of a situation that typically send your anxiety levels through the roof.

To comprehend fully how confronting thoughts works in CBT, consider the following example: Stacy doesn't want to take the subway because she fears she might faint and everyone will think she's crazy. She is asked by her therapist to write down her negative thoughts and locate the errors in her thinking – or cognitive distortion – and figure out a more sensible interpretation. Here are the results:

Negative thought #1: What if I faint on the subway?

Cognitive distortion: Being as pessimistic as possible

More rational thought: I've never fainted in my entire life, so there is very little chance that it will happen on the subway.

Negative thought #2: If I faint, it will be awful!

Cognitive distortion: Sensationalizing the possible outcome

More rational thought: If I do pass out, I will immediately be helped by other passengers. That's not so bad.

Negative thought #3: People will think I'm insane

Cognitive distortion:

Excepting the worst from people

More realistic thought:

More rational thought: People will feel sympathy for me if I fall.

Substituting negative thoughts with more rational ones is not as easy as it seems. Typically, negative thoughts arise from a lifetime of thinking patterns. It takes time to break this conditioning. This is why CBT consists of doing homework as well as regular therapy. CBT may also include:

- Learning to realize when your anxiety is kicking in and what sensations in your body are giving it off.

- Learning coping and relaxation skills to combat anxiety and panic symptoms.

- Facing and conquering your fears (first in your imagination than in real life).

Another way to aid your own anxiety therapy is by leading a more positive lifestyle. Your anxiety is affected by everything from your workload to your social life. Roll out the carpet for success by making conscious decisions that encourage relaxation, vigor, and an optimistic outlook in your daily activities.

Build your connections with others

Solitude and self-isolation are the perfect combinations for anxiety. Lower your susceptibility by connecting with others. Commit to seeing friends; partake in support groups; let your loved ones know your concerns and worries.

Take up healthy lifestyle habits

Physical endurance reduces anxiety and tension, so add some regular exercise into your daily routine. Don't use drugs and alcohol to deal with your symptoms and attempt to stay away from stimulants, like excessive coffee and cigarettes, which can boost your anxiety.

Lower stress in your life

Analyze the stress in your life and seek ways to reduce it. Stay away from individuals who trigger your anxiety, say no to overworking, and open your daily schedule up to some fun and relaxation time.

THE ABCD Model

Overview of the A-B-C-D model in the context of anger management

The ABCD model is a CBT technique created by Dr. Albert Ellis, a Psychologist, and member of the American Board of Professional Psychology. When used properly, this technique can help manage a range of emotional issues, including anger management problems.

Below is a summary of the ABCD CBT model, using anger as the problem focal point:

A = Activating Event

This indicates the activating event or "trigger" of your anger.

B = Belief System

Your belief system indicates how you exhibit the triggering event (A). What goes through your mind about the event? What are your beliefs as to how others should conduct themselves?

C = Consequences

This indicates what your feelings are and how you react according to your belief system, in other words, the behavioral and emotional consequences that arise from A + B. When angry, it's not uncommon to experience other sensations, like fear, since anger is an interconnected emotion.

Other "consequences" might include small physical variations, like storming out of an altercation or contemplating doing emotional damage to others. More severe behavioral reactions might include name-calling, yelling, and threats of physical violence.

D = Dispute

D indicates a very important part of the anger management process: the self-reflection of your beliefs and expectations. Are they irrational or unrealistic? If so, what might be a more moderate alternative way to connect with the situation? By "disputing" those impulsive reactions to the situation, you can take a more balanced and rational approach, which can assist you in controlling your anger.

Example of the A-B-C-D Model

Below is an example illustrating how this model can be incorporated into anger management:

A = Activating Event

Let's say you are commuting to work and another driver cuts you off, almost resulting in a collision. You are overwhelmed with both the stress of running late to work and almost getting into a life-threatening situation.

You tell yourself, "Why would anyone drive like that?" "Everybody on the road these days drives recklessly," "I'm a very considerate driver. I would never do that," "If I got hit because of that driver's decisions, I would not make it on time to work, and I could have been seriously injured."

C = Consequences

After the triggering incident (i.e., being cut off by another driver), you proceed to shout out an exploitive at the driver as a way to get even. You notice your body becomes tense, your heart starts racing, and you feel like you will not be satisfied until you get your revenge.

D = Dispute

As a reaction to the trigger situation and its sequence, rather than validating your anger impulses, you could alter your thinking to negate them (this is the "D" dispute part of the treatment). For example, you can brush aside the event by telling yourself: "It's a shame that some people are so reckless on the road, but that's just the way the world is. Most people are law-abiding and courteous drivers, and I am grateful for that as well," or "That was a close call, but even if my car got slightly damaged, I would have still been able to make it work and would have easily been able to prove the events to my boss as to avoid any further trouble at work."

By using this type of level-headed self-talk, you will have a greater chance to diffuse the anger a bit and help you get your emotions in check.

How to apply this model to anger management

The first step in controlling your anger management with this tool is to boost your awareness of the incident in the following steps:

A) Identify the triggering point of the anger.

B) Reflect upon how the triggering event affected you (e.g., what were your thoughts when it happened).

C) Identify all the related behavioral and emotional reactions that concurred.

Due to the fact that our minds work so quickly, we can arrive at C – consequences – very rapidly. So, to apply this tool correctly, you should analyze the prior events that resulted in triggering your anger by writing down the incidents on your worksheet.

You can use this table below as a guideline to the ABCD system

Taking the time to record these events can help you drill some solutions into your subconscious mind so that during the heat of the moment, you will be ready to act accordingly. Essentially, you are practicing how to control your anger when you examine past events and work out more positive solutions that can diffuse the situation, instead of cranking up your anger.

The reflective process helps you rewire your thinking process by boosting your pattern awareness and finding ways to react to them in a more positive manner. For example, you might begin to notice that (incomplete)

How Dialectical Behavior Therapy Can Help CBT Patients

Dialectical behavior therapy (DBT) is a type of Cognitive Behavioral Therapy. Its purpose is to teach people how to cope with stress healthfully, be present in the moment, control emotions, and improve their relationships with others.

It was initially meant to help people with Borderline Personality Disorder (BPD) but was later adjusted for other conditions where the patient displays self-destructive behavior, such as substance abuse and eating disorders. It is also often used in therapy to help reduce symptoms of post-traumatic stress disorder (PTSD).

History

DBT was conceived as a modified form of Cognitive Behavioral Therapy (CBT) in the mid 1980s by Dr. Marsha Linehan and her workmates after they noticed that CBT by itself did not yield the expected results in patients with BPD. Dr. Linehan and her colleagues included techniques and created a treatment that catered to the special needs of those patients.

She decided to integrate the added techniques into her practice. Dr. Linehan and her team had a lot of challenges after running tests on the relative effectiveness of CBT in a specific population. She discovered three significant issues with the exertion of standard CBT:

Participants felt weakened after the change-focused interventions were done. These feelings usually resulted in participants pulling back from the therapy, showing resentment toward therapists, or a combination of both extremes.

Therapists and participants recreated a reinforcement pattern in which productivity was hindered and redirection and avoidance were encouraged. When therapists insisted on change, participants became angered. When therapists allowed a change in subject, participants became joyful and gave positive feedback. This vortex bewildered both the participant and therapist into thinking that everything was going well, when in reality, the opposite was happening.

Due to the severity of emotional crisis situations, therapists strongly emphasize safety concerns during therapy, such as hostile gestures towards the therapist, suicidal thoughts, or self-injurious behavior. Often, teaching coping skills or discussing behavioral functioning becomes an issue of low priority.

After researching these problems, Dr. Linehan created various adaptations to CBT. These instantly addressed the necessities of the population. To ensure participants felt validated and supported, acceptance-based techniques were integrated before they were asked to prioritize change.

Additionally, dialects were included to give therapists and participants the chance to focus on the fundamentals of polar opposites, such as tolerance and change.

In 1993, Dr. Linehan published her first treatment manual, titled *Cognitive Behavioral Treatment of Borderline Personality Disorder*, which resulted in a huge boost in popularity for CBT. Over the last three decades, a vast number of studies have supported the effectiveness of DBT. In fact, DBT is currently practiced in dozens of countries worldwide and is approved by SAMHSA's Registry of Evidence-Based Practices.

Dialectical behavior therapy consists of the idea that Borderline Personality Disorder is caused by two important factors:

- You are highly vulnerable emotionally – for example, any slight amount of stress makes you intensely anxious.

- Your upbringing was in an environment where your emotions were invalidated by your caregivers or siblings, e.g., a parent may have treated your emotional outbursts as you "being silly" even if it was your anxiety kicking in.

The result of these 2 factors may mean you will become engulfed in a vortex where you experience overwhelming depressing emotions, yet question your own sanity for having said emotions. You automatically think there is something wrong with you because you were assured so growing up. These thoughts result in more upsetting emotions.

The purpose of DBT is to take you out of the vortex by applying 2 important concepts:

- Validation: Recognizing your emotions are justified, acceptable, and real.

Your DBT therapist will focus on bringing positive changes in your behavior using both of these concepts. For example, your therapist may explain to you why your feelings of overwhelming depression are valid and that acting in self-harm because of that does not make you a crazy or bad person.

However, the therapist will then insist that self-harm is not the right way to deal with your feelings of sadness or depression. The objective of DBT is to steer your mind away from seeing the experiences in your life through the lens of a narrow and rigid viewpoint that leads you to commit harmful acts to yourself.

DBT typically consists of weekly group or individual sessions, and you'll be granted access to your therapist's out of office number in case you are having an emotional crisis. DBT works best with teamwork. You need to make an effort to be cooperative with your therapist and peers in the group sessions, and likewise, the therapists cooperate as a team.

DBT is especially optimal for women who have a history of self-harm suicidal intentions. It's recommended by the National Institute for Health and Care Excellence (NICE) as the best treatment option for those women to try.

Dialectical Behavior Therapy Strategies

People who undergo DBT are trained to change their behavior favorably by learning four main strategies:

Core mindfulness

Mindfulness skills are arguably the most important technique in DBT. This skill emphasizes the importance of being in the present or "living in the moment". By accomplishing this, you can focus on paying attention to all the things happening internally (feelings, thoughts, impulses, sensations) as well as externally (things you see, smell, touch, and hear).

These skills will allow you to calm down, so you can concentrate on the necessary coping skills required to control emotional pain. Mindfulness can help you slow down and make smart decisions when you are caught in a situation that could possibly lead to a tense altercation.

Starting a mindfulness meditation practice

Practicing mindfulness meditation is an easy and straightforward process that anyone can do, but if you are having trouble following through, you can find a teacher or program to help you get on the right track, especially if you are doing meditation for mental health reasons.

Every bit of practice helps out a great deal. Here's a simple technique you can use to start on the right foot:

Find a comfortable and silent place. Sit down on a chair or down on the ground with your head and back upright and relaxed. It's also recommended to wear elastic and comfortable clothing that doesn't distract you.

1. Set aside all past and future thoughts and concentrate on the present.

2. Take control of your breath, attuning to the feeling of air flowing in and out of your body every time you breathe. Feel the air enter your nostrils and leave your mouth as your belly falls and rises. Focus on each breath and how they are changing.

3. See every idea come in and out, whether it be anxiety, fear or hope. When you come up with a thought, don't ignore or restrain it. Simply notice it, stay calm, and control it with your breath.

Distress tolerance

Distress tolerance emphasizes the importance of self-love and appreciating your current situation. To be more precise, you are taught how to deal with crises in the healthiest way possible using four techniques: diversion, self-soothing, movement, and assessing the pros and cons. By practicing distress tolerance techniques, you will learn to be ready to confront any intense emotions and cope with them with a positive state of mind and outlook.

Interpersonal effectiveness

Interpersonal effectiveness is meant to help boost your assertiveness in a relationship (e.g.., making demands and saying "no") intelligently and keeping that relationship healthy and positive. This occurs by listening and communicating more effectively, always looking for a smart way to deal with difficult people, and treating yourself and others with respect.

Emotion regulation

Emotion regulation teaches you the skills required to keep your emotional system functioning and healthy. It trains you on how to decrease the intensity of your emotions and how to react to them properly when you have them. By acknowledging and coping with pessimistic emotions, such as anger, you can decrease your emotional fragility and give yourself more favorable emotional experiences.

Catastrophizing

Catastrophizing is a type of distorted thinking that drastically increases anxiety, causing us to fear the worst possible outcome or perceive small events as a crisis.

The mind of a catastrophizer looks at the challenges that face them with a defeatist mentality and expects the worst possible outcome.

Their minds are in a constant what-if state. This is when their minds are set off: What if my worst fears come true?

Catastrophizing usually consists of two types. In the first, it morphs a regular event and gives it a disastrous "spin". The second happens when we analyze the future and predict that everything is going to end badly. Getting out of this vortex can be hard; the good news with anxiety is there are a few simple steps you can take to defuse situations before they get out of control.

- Recognize when your mind is having negative thoughts.

- Start journaling your negative thoughts, as well as what happened and your thoughts about the events through as much of a neutral lens as you can, and finally write down how you reacted and what your behavior was.

- Switch your self-thoughts to being more hopeful and happy.

- Rather than trying to prevent your mind from catastrophizing in the near future (it's impossible to avoid), realize that sometimes the worst-case scenario in your current situation isn't always so bad.

Polarized thinking

Polarized thinking occurs when you think every outcome falls under a right or wrong category.

When you perceive matters in terms of purely bad or purely good, it results in unattainable standards and severe levels of stress.

Polarized thinking pops up when you suppress the hopes and positive thoughts of a particular event or outcome, such as applying for the college of your dreams, earning a specific amount of income, wanting to impress everyone, or just achieving a certain level of happiness.

- Realize that the spectrum between tragedy and triumph is a big one and that the majority of things fall somewhere in the middle.

- Understand that your future happiness is not going to be determined by a single accomplishment or failure in your life.

- Don't expect people to agree with you on everything or that your values will never change.

- Try to identify the real consequences of defeat and try to prepare yourself mentally to deal with those consequences.

Filtering

Filtering is magnifying the negative details while filtering out every positive facet of an event or situation.

For example, an individual might take a single, negative detail and focus on it entirely, so their vision ends up distorted through a darkened point of view.

- Learn to analyze things objectively and clearly, even if it makes you more conscious of the bad things.

- Look for positives.

- Find the positive side to every bad situation.

- Avoid "minimalizing" your attempts or accomplishments.

- Recognize your improvement process by comparing how you were doing things in the near and distant past.

Personalization

Personalization is believing that everything people say or do is out to hurt you in particular, for example, believing that a friend's tantrum is due to you agitating them at an earlier point when in reality they are reacting to something that just happened. People with this line of thinking also compare themselves to others as a way to evaluate who's better-looking, smarter, etc.

As a result, you are constantly urged to test your worth as a person by comparing yourself to others. If you are deemed as better, you feel momentary relief. However, if you are deemed less, you feel devastated. The logic behind this thinking pattern is that you see every situation, every conversation, as an indication of your own value and worth.

- Understand that not all people are self-aware enough to know that their bad moods are pouring out.

- Realize that other people can be going through a lot and be suppressing their emotions.

- If you truly believe you've hurt or offended someone – ask them.

- If your mind is drawing a blank, realize that you are probably suffering from personalization, but don't beat yourself over it. Evaluate it.

- Attempt to avoid putting all the blame on yourself before you analyze all the facts next time.

- Try not to alter your behavior when around a specific person: their mood is their problem.

Overgeneralizations

Overgeneralization is jumping to a broad conclusion as a result of a single anecdotal event or piece of evidence. If we experience something bad once, we expect the same result again and again.

A person may perceive a single bad experience as an endless pattern of defeat. Always using extremes such as "never" and "always" are usually hints that this kind of thinking is in effect.

This distortion can result in a limited life experience, as you reject future failures from fear that you will repeat the same result as a previous incident. You automatically assume things without anyone saying anything, as though you can read their feelings and the reasons they act out how they do. In particular, you feel you can determine what someone's feelings are towards you. For example, an individual might believe that someone is responding maliciously toward them and doesn't even make the attempt to see if they are correct.

- Analyze your tendency to generalize in your daily life.

- Next time, attempt to stick to the facts; is it actually "always" or "never" or are your emotions getting the better of you? Try to see it through a neutral lens as much as possible.

- Try to work on improving events in isolation, rather than seeing events in the past as a forecast of what will occur in the future.

Attribution errors

Similar to overgeneralizations, it's not rational to believe you can accurately know why a person is behaving the way they are. Their conduct may or may not be intentional.

The person might not even know that the things they are doing are wrong. Their actions might sometimes have an effect on you indirectly. Their conduct may have unintended results to others or may occur by happenstance.

Whether we like to admit it or not, we judge others on their behavior, and we judge ourselves on intention. Determining the cause when the effect of something can only be observed is a difficult task.

- Be careful of "consensus" information. If the majority of people act the same way when experiencing the same event, then the cause of the behavior is more than likely to be the event at hand.

- Ask yourself what your behavior would be in the same circumstance.

- Look for hard to see causes, especially ones from less-striking factors.

Simple steps to challenge cognitive distortions

Be mindful of the things you think about yourself. Ask yourself: "Are these thoughts to my benefit?" or "What is it that is upsetting me?"

Question your thoughts and keep in mind that just because you believe something is true doesn't mean it is. Ask yourself: "Am I being rational?" "Would others in my circumstance think these same thoughts?" "Is this my mind stuck in a cognitive distortion vortex?"

Consider the strategies below and ask yourself these questions:

- Go with the evidence: Where is the evidence that proves or disproves my thoughts? Am I nitpicking only the negatives and dismissing other information? "Am I overgeneralizing without checking for facts first?"

- Seek alternative answers: "Do other answers possibly exist? Is there another perspective to look at this from? Am I being too narrow-minded?"

- "What are some more positive thoughts?" "What thoughts can I embrace to help me stay calm and achieve the best outcome in this situation?"

Overgeneralizations can debilitate those who suffer from social anxiety, hindering your social interactions and preventing you from achieving your goals. However, with some mental reframing, you can control your symptoms and cure your social anxiety.

Mindful Thinking for Cognitive Behavioral Therapy

We all know people who are masterful at controlling their emotions. They don't let stressful situations get to them. They're excellent at making decisions under pressure, and they know how to find a solution. Regardless of their good qualities, however, they're also honest when it comes to analyzing themselves. They handle criticism well and know how to apply it to improve their lives.

Is this the type of person you would aspire to be?

As time goes on, more people acknowledge that mindful thinking is a major factor in achieving professional success; businesses are increasingly prioritizing it in their hiring and promoting practices.

So, what is mindful thinking, and how can you improve yours?

Every person has a unique and special personality, different necessities and habits, and different ways of expressing ourselves. Committing to this requires tact and cunningness – especially if we aspire to be successful in life. Mindful thinking will play an important role.

Why are people who use mindful thinking usually successful in everything they apply themselves to? Because they're a necessary part of every team. When individuals with high mindful thinking abilities make a request, it gets answered. When they call out for help, they receive it. Because they have the ability to make others respect them, their experience in life is much easier than those who are easily angered.

Characteristics of a mindful thinker

- Self-Awareness

- Individuals with high mindful thinking are typically also very self-aware. They are in touch with their emotions, and due to this, they don't allow their emotions to dominate them. They're assertive – because they believe in their intuition and don't allow their feelings to get out of control.

- Likewise, they are capable of making an honest evaluation of themselves. They are familiar with their weaknesses and strengths, and they try to improve these aspects in their life, so they can become more productive. Many people think this trait is the most important aspect of mindful thinking.

Self-Regulation – Individuals who self-regulate usually don't allow anger or jealousy to overtake them. They also do not make careless, impulsive decisions. They are known for being very careful with their decisions when the moment calls for it.

Traits of self-regulation are mindfulness, the ability to adapt and change, integrity, and the discipline to say no.

Motivation – Individuals who use a high amount of mindful thinking live their lives constantly motivated. They're capable of deferring instant results for long-term success. They love to be challenged, productive, and do their work in an efficient manner.

Empathy – This is arguable the second-most significant factor of mindful thinking. People with empathy are able to sympathize with the needs, wants, and viewpoints of people around them. Empathetic people are blessed with the ability to recognize the emotions of others, even if those emotions are suppressed. As a result, people with empathy are typically great at listening, managing relationships, and connecting with others.

Social skills – It's relatively easy to have a conversation with people with high social skills, a trait that comes with high mindful thinking. Those who possess good social skills are usually team players. Instead of prioritizing their own success first, they strive to help other people grow and shine. They can defuse confrontations, are great communicators, and are experts in building and managing relationships.

How to improve your mindful thinking abilities

If you would like the same benefits as the people mentioned above, then there is good news! Any person can learn mindful thinking through practice. As well as the skills in the previously mentioned areas, here are some strategies to help you get started learning how to be emotionally intelligent:

Pay attention to the way you react to people. Do you make rash decisions before you consider the consequences? Do you pre-judge people? Take a good look at what you think of other people and how you interact with them. Try putting yourself in their shoes and keep an open mind when hearing their perspectives and needs.

Look around at your workplace. Do you look for validation for your achievements? Humility is an amazing quality, and it doesn't imply that you lack self-confidence or are shy. When you embrace humility, you acknowledge that you are aware of what you did and you can silently be confident about it. Give other people a chance to be the center of attention – put the spotlight on them and try not to care so much about the praise of others.

Do a self-evaluation. What do you see as your weaknesses? Are you willing to acknowledge your flaws and how you could improve on them to grow into a better person? Do some deep thinking and look at yourself through a neutral lens – It can be a life-changing experience.

Analyze how stressful situations impact you. Does a long delay or failure in things going your way make you upset? Do you project the blame to others even when it's not their fault? Being able to remain calm and collected in stressful situations is a highly valued skill – both in the business world and in social life. Be aware of your emotions and keep them under control during a crisis.

Take responsibility for your errors. If you slighted someone you love, apologize sincerely – don't brush it aside or evade the person. People are a lot more forgiving than you probably think, and an honest attempt to correct things always makes people feel appreciated.

Evaluate how your actions impact other people – any time you are about to take those actions. If you do believe it will impact others, imagine how you would feel in their place. Would you like to be treated that way? If you have no choice but to take that action, how can you balance the action out to have the least painful effect possible on that person?

Conclusion

Mindful thinking skills are essential for good social communication. Research has shown that this ability is more indicative of achieving success in life than IQ alone. The good news is that there are many ways that you can do to increase your own personal and social mindful thinking. Getting to know your own emotions can be the key factor in improving your communication skills, well-being, and even relationships.

There you have it. You are now well on your way to finally achieving peace of mind through the power of Cognitive Behavioral Therapy!

Be prepared to live a life filled with positivity, feel great and achieve the goals you always strived for in life! Thank you for taking the time to read my book and stay tuned for more books on self-help in the future.

If you enjoyed my book and would recommend it to anyone. I'd be very grateful if you can leave a short review on Amazon. Your feedback is really important, and I will use the opportunity to further improve this book even more in the future.

Thanks again for your support!